FOREWORD

My poems, at Mammon's grim behest,
Have been collected here by Crest.
Forgive them if they seem too thin;
Diaphanousness is no sin
In ballerinas' skirts, so why
My own transparency decry?
It pleased me once to write them, and
I'm pleased to place them in your hand.

by John Updike

THE POORHOUSE FAIR, *a novel*

THE SAME DOOR, *short stories*

RABBIT, RUN, *a novel*

PIGEON FEATHERS *and other stories*

THE CENTAUR, *a novel*

VERSE:
THE CARPENTERED HEN
and other tame creatures

TELEPHONE POLES *and other poems*

John Updike

VERSE

THE CARPENTERED HEN
and other tame creatures

TELEPHONE POLES
and other poems

A CREST REPRINT

FAWCETT PUBLICATIONS, INC., GREENWICH, CONN.
MEMBER OF AMERICAN BOOK PUBLISHERS COUNCIL, INC.

THE CARPENTERED HEN and other tame creatures
is reprinted in this volume by arrangement with Harper & Row,
Publishers. TELEPHONE POLES and other poems is reprinted
by arrangement with Alfred A. Knopf, Inc.

Copyright © 1954, 1955, 1956, 1957, 1958, 1959, 1960, 1961,
1962, 1963 by John Updike.
Foreword copyright © 1965 by John Updike

Eighty-nine of these poems were originally published in
The New Yorker. Other poems were first printed in
Harper's Magazine, The Commonweal, The New Republic,
The Christian Century, American Scholar, Punch, The Ladies' Home
Journal, What's New, Syracuse 10, and The Harvard Lampoon.

"The One-Year-Old" first appeared in the March, 1957, issue of
The Ladies' Home Journal.
Copyright © 1957 by The Curtis Publishing Company.

Library of Congress Catalog Card Number: 65-12882

First Crest printing, February 1965

Crest Books are published by Fawcett World Library,
67 West 44th Street, New York, N. Y. 10036.
Printed in the United States of America.

CONTENTS

THE CARPENTERED HEN
and other tame creatures

TELEPHONE POLES
and other poems

I

II

John Updike

VERSE

THE CARPENTERED HEN

and other tame creatures

(1958)

TO MARY
with love

DUET, WITH MUFFLED BRAKE DRUMS

50 Years Ago Rolls met Royce—a Meeting that
made Engineering History
                    —*advertisement in The New Yorker*

Where gray walks slope through shadows shaped like lace
Down to dimpleproof ponds, a precious place
Where birds of porcelain sing as with one voice
Two gold and velvet notes—there Rolls met Royce.

"Hallo," said Rolls. His umber silhouette
Seemed mounted on a blotter brushed when wet
To indicate a park. Beyond, a brown
Line hinted at the profile of The Town.

And Royce, his teeth and creases straight, his eye
A perfect match for that well-lacquered sky
(Has zenith since, or iris, been so pure?),
Responded, "Pleased to meet you, I am sure."

A graceful pause, then Rolls, the taller, spake:
"Ah—is there anything you'd care to make?
A day of it? A fourth at bridge? Some tea?"
Royce murmured, "If your afternoon is free,
I'd rather, much, make engineering history."

EX-BASKETBALL PLAYER

Pearl Avenue runs past the high-school lot,
Bends with the trolley tracks, and stops, cut off
Before it has a chance to go two blocks,
At Colonel McComsky Plaza. Berth's Garage
Is on the corner facing west, and there,
Most days, you'll find Flick Webb, who helps Berth out.

Flick stands tall among the idiot pumps—
Five on a side, the old bubble-head style,
Their rubber elbows hanging loose and low.
One's nostrils are two S's, and his eyes
An E and O. And one is squat, without
A head at all—more of a football type.

Once Flick played for the high-school team, the Wizards.
He was good: in fact, the best. In '46
He bucketed three hundred ninety points,
A county record still. The ball loved Flick.
I saw him rack up thirty-eight or forty
In one home game. His hands were like wild birds.

He never learned a trade, he just sells gas,
Checks oil, and changes flats. Once in a while,
As a gag, he dribbles an inner tube,
But most of us remember anyway.
His hands are fine and nervous on the lug wrench.
It makes no difference to the lug wrench, though.

Off work, he hangs around Mae's luncheonette.
Grease-gray and kind of coiled, he plays pinball,
Smokes thin cigars, and nurses lemon phosphates.
Flick seldom says a word to Mae, just nods
Beyond her face toward bright applauding tiers
Of Necco Wafers, Nibs, and Juju Beads.

PLAYER PIANO

My stick fingers click with a snicker
And, chuckling, they knuckle the keys;
Light-footed, my steel feelers flicker
And pluck from these keys melodics.

My paper can caper; abandon
Is broadcast by dint of my din,
And no man or band has a hand in
The tones I turn on from within.

At times I'm a jumble of rumbles,
At others I'm light like the moon,
But never my numb plunker fumbles,
Misstrums me, or tries a new tune.

SHIPBORED

That line is the horizon line.
The blue above it is divine.
The blue below it is marine.
Sometimes the blue below is green.

Sometimes the blue above is gray,
Betokening a cloudy day.
Sometimes the blue below is white,
Foreshadowing a windy night.

Sometimes a drifting coconut
Or albatross adds color, but
The blue above is mostly blue.
The blue below and I are, too.

AN ODE

FIRED INTO BEING BY LIFE'S 48-STAR EDITORIAL,
"WANTED: AN AMERICAN NOVEL"

STROPHE

*Ours is the most powerful nation in the world. It has had a
decade of unparalleled prosperity. Yet it is still producing a
literature which sounds sometimes as if it were written by
an unemployed homosexual. . . .*

ANTISTROPHE

I'm going to write a novel, hey,
    I'll write it as per *Life*:
I'm going to say "What a splendid day"
    And "How I love my wife!"
Let heroines be once again
    Pink, languid, soft, and tall,
For from my pen shall flow forth men
    Heterosexual.

STROPHE

*Atomic fear or not, the incredible accomplishments of our
day are surely the raw stuff of saga.*

ANTISTROPHE

Raw stuff shall be the stuff of which
    My saga will be made:
Brown soil, black pitch, the lovely rich,
    The noble poor, the raid
On Harpers Ferry, Bunker Hill,
    Forefathers fairly met,
The home, the mill, the hearth, the Bill
    Of Rights, et cet., et cet.

STROPHE

Nobody wants a Pollyanna literature.

ANTISTROPHE

I shan't play Pollyanna, no,
    I'll stare facts in the eye:
Folks come and go, experience woe,
    And, when they're tired, die.
Unflinchingly, I plan to write
    A book to comprehend
Rape, fury, spite, and, burning bright,
    A sunset at The End.

STROPHE

*In every healthy man there is a wisdom deeper than his
conscious mind, reaching beyond memory to the primeval
rivers, a yea-saying to the goodness and joy of life.*

ANTISTROPHE

A wise and not unhealthy man,
    I'm telling everyone
That deeper than the old brainpan
    Primeval rivers run;
For *Life* is joy and *Time* is gay
    And *Fortune* smiles on those
Good books that say, at some length, "Yea,"
    And thereby spite the Noes.

THE CLAN

Emlyn reads in Dickens' clothes.
Tennessee writes fleshy prose;
William Carlos, bony poems.
Esther swims in hippodromes.
Ted likes hits but hates his fans;
Gluyas draws Americans.
Vaughan pens music, score on score;
Soapy is a governor.
I trust everybody is
Thankful for the Williamses.

WHY THE TELEPHONE WIRES DIP AND THE POLES ARE CRACKED AND CROOKED

The old men say
young men in gray
hung this thread across our plains
acres and acres ago.

But we, the enlightened, know
in point of fact it's what remains
of the flight of a marvellous crow
no one saw:
Each pole, a caw.

THE POPULATION OF ARGENTINA
[with T.D.E., 1952]

The Rand McNally Co.:
How little does it know!
  How much those clerks have missed
  Who blithely list
Argentina's pop. as four-
Teen million, and no more,
  And even slightly less!
Why, I can count
Twice that amount
  By skimming through the columns of the daily press.

For every new edition
  Sees another harried soul
Seek a haven from sedition,
  Flee assassins, jump parole,
Or escape a harsh decision
  Of the anti-vice patrol
    By visiting that vast arena
    Of refugees called Argentina.

On the pampas, it is certain,
Lounges Richard Haliburton,
Adolf Hitler, Martha Raye,
Leon Trotsky's ex-valet,
Greta Garbo, Mildred Fletcher,
"Fingers" Pico—you can betcher
Bottom dollar they are there,
Inhaling *bueno* air,
    As well
As all the aunts of Sun Yat-sen,
    The ten
Lost Tribes of Israel,
    Side by side
With every Balkan prince who never died.

Rand, recount; recount, McNally:
There's been some slip-up in your tally;
    Count Argentinian heads again.
Search every cellar, scan each alley,
And you'll discover Axis Sally
    Playing poker with Hart Crane.

EVEN EGRETS ERR

Egregious was the egret's error, very.
   Egressing from a swamp, the bird eschewed
No egriot (a sour kind of cherry)*
   It saw, and reaped extremest egritude.§

* Obs.
§ Rare form of obs. Aegritude, meaning sickness.

SCENIC

O when in San Francisco do
As natives do: they sit and stare
And smile and stare again. The view
Is visible from anywhere.

Here hills are white with houses whence,
Across a multitude of sills,
The owners, lucky residents,
See other houses, other hills.

The meanest San Franciscan knows,
No matter what his past has been,
There are a thousand patios
Whose view he is included in.

The Golden Gate, the cable cars,
Twin Peaks, the Spreckels habitat,
The local ocean, sun, and stars—
When fog falls, one admires *that*.

Here homes are stacked in such a way
That every picture window has
An unmarred prospect of the Bay
And, in its center, Alcatraz.

TUNE, IN AMERICAN TYPE

Set and printed in Great Britain by Tonbridge
Printers, Ltd., Peach Hall Works, Tonbridge, in
Times nine on ten point, on paper made by John
Dickenson at Croxley, and bound by James Burn
at Esher.

> *—colophon in a book published by*
> *Michael Joseph (London)*

Ah, to be set and printed in
Great Britain now that Tonbridge Printers, Limited, employ old John
Dickenson, at Croxley. On
his pages is Times nine-on-ten-
point type impressed, and, lastly, when
at Peach Hall Works the job is done,
James Burn at Esher's job's begun.

Hey nonny nonny nonny,
Hey nonny nonny nay!

Tonbridge! Croxley! Esher! Ah,
is there, in America,
a tome contrived in such sweet towns?
No. English, English are the downs
where Jim Burn, honest craftsman, winds
beneath his load of reams; he binds
the sheets that once John Dickenson
squeezed flat from British pulp. *Hey non-*
ny nonny, etc.

LAMENT, FOR COCOA

The scum has come.
  My cocoa's cold.
The cup is numb,
  And I grow old.

It seems an age
  Since from the pot
It bubbled, beige
  And burning hot—

Too hot to be
  Too quickly quaffed.
Accordingly,
  I found a draft

And in it placed
  The boiling brew
And took a taste
  Of toast or two.

Alas, time flies
  And minutes chill;
My cocoa lies
  Dull brown and still.

How wearisome!
  In likelihood,
The scum, once come,
  Is come for good.

RECITATIVE FOR PUNISHED PRODUCTS

I was once a tire. To bolster sales
My cunning maker filled me full of nails.
My treads were shredded. I was made a flat
By great machines designed to do just that.

I was a typewriter. Harsh was my test.
Ten years I toiled unoiled without a rest.
One billion times, so claim the pedagogues,
The quick brown foxes jumped my lazy cogs.

I used to be a watch. My tick and tock
Were interchanged by polychronic shock.
The bit of bounce my spring retained was sapped
By tales of clocks alarmed, of watches strapped.

I am a shears. My thin lips prophesy
The Day to Come when angles cloud the sky,
When rugs rise up, mute tools get out of hand,
And crazed computers walk the frenzied land.

All:

Awesome the clangs will be, fearful the whirs
When products punish manufacturers.

V. B. NIMBLE, V. B. QUICK

Science, Pure and Applied, by V. B. Wigglesworth,
F.R.S., Quick Professor of Biology in the University of Cambridge.
        —a talk listed in the B.B.C. Radio Times

V. B. Wigglesworth wakes at noon,
Washes, shaves, and very soon
Is at the lab; he reads his mail,
Tweaks a tadpole by the tail,
Undoes his coat, removes his hat,
Dips a spider in a vat
Of alkaline, phones the press,
Tells them he is F. R. S.,
Subdivides six protocells,
Kills a rat by ringing bells,
Writes a treatise, edits two
Symposia on "Will Man Do?,"
Gives a lecture, audits three,
Has the Sperm Club in for tea,
Pensions off an aging spore,
Cracks a test tube, takes some pure
Science and applies it, finds
His hat, adjusts it, pulls the blinds,
Instructs the jellyfish to spawn,
And, by one o'clock, is gone.

SONG OF THE OPEN FIREPLACE

When silly Sol in winter roisters
And roasts us in our closed-up cloisters
Like hosts of out-of-season oysters,
    The logs glow red.

When Sol grows cool and solely caters
To polar bears and figure skaters
And homes are turned refrigerators,
    The flames are dead.

And when idyllically transpires
The merger every man desires
Of air that nips and wood that fires,
    It's time for bed.

MARCH: A BIRTHDAY POEM
for Elizabeth

My child as yet unborn, the doctors nod,
Agreeing that your first month shall be March,
A time of year I know by heart and like
To talk about—I too was born in March.

March, like November a month largely unloved,
Parades before April, who steals all shows
With his harlequinade of things renewed.
Impatient for that pastel fool's approach,
Our fathers taunted March, called him *Hlyd-monath*,
Though the month is mild, and a murmurer.
Indeed, after the Titan's fall and shatter
Of February, March seems a silence.
The Romans, finding February's ruins
At the feet of March, heard his wind as boasting
And hailed his guilt with a war-god's name.

As above some street in a cobbled sea-town
From opposing walls two huge boards thrust
To advertise two inns, so do the signs
Of Pisces the Fish and Aries the Ram
Overhang March. Depending on the day,
Your fortunate gem shall be the bloodstone
Or the diamond, your lucky color crimson
Or silver gray. You shall prove affable,
Impulsive, lucky in your friends, or cross,
According to the counterpoint of stars.
So press your business ventures, wear cravats,
And swear not by the moon. If you plant wheat,
Do it at dawn. The same for barley. Let
The tide transplant kohlrabi, leeks, and beans.
Toward the month's end, sow hardy annuals.

It was this month when Caesar fell, Stalin died,
And Beethoven. In this month snowflakes melt—
Those last dry crusts that huddle by the barn.
Now kites and crocuses are hoisted up.
Doors slap open. Dogs snuffle soggy leaves,
Rehearsing rusty repertoires of smells.
The color of March is the one that lies
On the shadow side of young tree trunks.

March is no land of extremes. Dull as life,
It offers small flowers and minor holidays.
Clouds stride sentry and hold our vision down.
By much the same token, agonized roots
Are hidden by earth. Much, much is opaque.
The thunder bluffs, wind cannot be gripped,
And kites and crocuses are what they are.
Still, child, it is far from a bad month,
For all its weight of compromise and hope.
As modest as a monk, March shall be there
When on that day without a yesterday
You, red and blind and blank, gulp the air.

SUNFLOWER

Sunflower, of flowers
the most lonely,
yardstick of hours,
long-term stander
in empty spaces,
shunner of bowers,
indolent bender
seldom, in only
the sharpest of showers:
tell us, why
is it your face is
a snarl of jet swirls
and gold arrows, a burning
old lion face high
in a cornflower sky,
yet by turning
your head, we find
you wear a girl's
bonnet behind?

POETESS

At verses she was not inept,
  Her feet were neatly numbered.
She never cried, she softly wept,
  She never slept, she slumbered.

She never ate and rarely dined,
  Her tongue found sweetmeats sour.
She never guessed, but oft divined
  The secrets of a flower.

A flower! Fragrant, pliant, clean,
  More dear to her than crystal.
She knew what yearnings dozed between
  The stamen and the pistil.

Dawn took her thither to the wood,
  At even, home she hithered.
Ah, to the gentle Pan is good—
  She never died, she withered.

POOEM

Writing here last autumn of my hopes of seeing
a hoopoe . . .
   —*Sir Stephen Tallents in the London Times*

I, too, once hoped to have a hoopoe
Wing its way within my scoopoe,
Crested, quick, and heliotroopoe,
   Proud *Upupa epops*.
   For what seemed an eternity,
I sat upon a grassy sloopoe,
Gazing through a telescoopoe,
Weaving snares of finest roopoe,
   Fit for *Upupa epops*.
   At last, one day, there came to me,
Inside a crusty enveloopoe,
This note: "Abandon hope, you doopoe;
The hoopoe is a misanthroopoe.
   (Signed) Your far-off friend, *U. e.*"

CAPACITY

CAPACITY 26 PASSENGERS
—sign in a bus

Affable, bibulous,
corpulent, dull,
eager-to-find-a-seat,
formidable,
garrulous, humorous,
icy, jejune,
knockabout, laden-
with-luggage (maroon),
mild-mannered, narrow-necked,
oval-eyed, pert,
querulous, rakish,
seductive, tart, vert-
iginous, willowy,
xanthic (or yellow),
young, zebuesque are my
passengers fellow.

AN IMAGINABLE CONFERENCE

MR. HENRY GREEN, INDUSTRIALIST, AND MR.
WALLACE STEVENS, VICE-PRESIDENT OF THE
HARTFORD ACCIDENT & INDEMNITY CO., MEET IN
THE COURSE OF BUSINESS

Exchanging gentle grips, the men retire,
prologued by courteous bumbling at the door,
retreat to where a rare room deep exists
on an odd floor, subtly carpeted. The walls

wear charts like checkered vests and blotters ape
the green of cricket fields. Glass multiplies
the pausing men to twice infinity.
An inkstand of blue marble has been carven:

no young girl's wrist is more discreetly veined.
An office boy misplaced and slack intrudes,
apologizes speaking without commas
"Oh sorry sirs I thought" which signifies

what wellmeant wimbly wambly stuff it is
we seem to be made of. Beyond the room,
a gander sun's pure rhetoric ferments
imbroglios of bloom. The stone is so.

The pair confers in murmurings, with words
select and Sunday-soft. No more is known,
but rumor goes that as they hatched the deal,
vistas of lilac weighted their shrewd lids.

THE STORY OF MY LIFE

Fernando Valenti, enthusiast, Yale graduate, and himself represented by numerous recordings of Scarlatti.

—Saturday Review

Enthused I went to Yale, enthused
I graduated. Still infused
With this enthusiasm when
Scarlatti called, I answered en-
Thusiastically, and thus
I made recordings numerous,
So numerous that I am classed,
Quite simply, as "enthusiast."

THE NEWLYWEDS

After a one-day honeymoon, the Fishers rushed
off to a soft drink bottlers' convention, then on
to a ball game, a TV rehearsal and a movie pre-
view.

—Life

"We're married," said Eddie.
Said Debbie, "Incredi-

ble! When is our honey-
moon?" "Over and done," he

replied. "Feeling logy?
Drink Coke." "Look at Yogi

go!" Debbie cried. "Groovy!"
"Rehearsal?" "The movie."

"Some weddie," said Debbie.
Said Eddie, "Yeah, mebbe."

HUMANITIES COURSE

Professor Varder handles Dante
  With wry respect; while one can see
It's all a lie, one must admit
  The "beauty" of the "imagery."

Professor Varder slyly smiles,
  Describing Hegel as a "sage;"
But still, the man has value—he
  Reflects the "temper" of his "age."

Montaigne, Tom Paine, St. Augustine:
  Although their notions came to naught,
They still are "crucial figures" in
  The "pageantry" of "Western thought."

ENGLISH TRAIN COMPARTMENT

These faces make a chapel where worship comes easy:
Homo enim naturaliter est animal sociale.

The flutter of a *Guardian,* the riveted image
of Combe-in-Teignhead, faded by decades of eyes,
the sting of smoke, the coughs, the whispering
lend flavor to piety's honest bone.

Half-sick, we suck our teeth, consult our thumbs,
through brown-stained glass confront the barbered hills
and tailored trees of a tame and castrate land.
Sheep elegant enough for any eclogue
browse under Constable clouds. The unnatural
darkness swells, and passengers stir
at the sound of tapping fingernails. Rain,
beginning, hyphenates our racing windows.

Hands and smiles are freed by the benediction's close.
The lights, always on, now tell. One man talks,
and the water, sluicing sideways, teases our direction.
Indeed, we are lively, smug, and brave
as adventurers safe after some great hazard,
while beside our shoulders the landscape streams
as across the eye of a bathysphere surfacing.

TIME'S FOOL

Frederick Alexander Pott
arrives at parties on the dot.
The drinks have not been mixed, the wife
is still applying, with a knife,
extract of shrimp and chicken spread
to parallelograms of bread
when Pott appears, remarking, "I'm
afraid I'm barging in on time."

Frederick Pott is never late
for any rendezvous or date.
Arrange to meet at some hotel;
you'll find he's been there since the bell
tolled the appointed hour. Not
intending to embarrass, Pott
says shyly, "Punctuality
is psychological with me."

Pott takes the most preposterous pains
to suit the scheduled times of trains.
He goes to concerts, races, plays,
allowing nicely for delays,
and at the age three score and ten
Pott plans to perish; doubtless then
he'll ask, as he has often done,
"This *was* the time agreed upon?"

PHILOLOGICAL

The British puss demurely mews;
His transatlantic kin meow.
The kine in Minnesota moo;
Not so the gentle Devon cows:
      They low,
As every school child ought to know.

TO AN USHERETTE

Ah come with me,
Petite chérie,
And we shall rather happy be.
I know a modest luncheonette
Where, for a little, one can get
A choplet, baby Lima beans,
And, segmented, two tangerines.

Le coup de grâce,
My petty lass,
Will be a demi-demitasse
Within a serviette conveyed
By weazened waiters, underpaid,
Who mincingly might grant us spoons
While a combo tinkles trivial tunes.

Ah with me come,
Ma faible femme,
And I shall say I love you some.

SUNGLASSES

On an olive beach, beneath a turquoise sky
And a limeade sun, by a lurid sea,
While the beryl clouds went blithely by,
We ensconced ourselves, my love and me.

O her verdant hair! and her aqua smile!
O my soul, afloat in an emerald bliss
That retained its tint all the watery while—
And her copper skin, all verdigris!

CLOUD SHADOWS
(New Hampshire)

I

That white coconut, the sun,
　is hidden by his blue leaves,
piratical great galleons.

Our sky their spanking sea,
　they thrust us to an ocean floor,
withal with certain courtesy.

II

These courtly cotton-bellies rub
　around the jewel we live within
and down to the muddled hub

drop complements.
　Down shafts of violet fall
counterweights of shadow, hence

brown, blue, and gray occur
　upon the chipmunk-colored
earth's fur.

III

Pine islands in a broken lake.
　Beyond Laconia the hills,
islanded by shadows, take

in cooling middle distance
　a motion from above, and lo!
grave mountains belly dance.

A MODEST MOUND OF BONES
(Pennsylvania)

That short-sleeved man, our
    uncle owns
the farm next our farm, south
    and west of us, and
he butchers for a living, hand-to-mouth.
    Once walking on his land
we found a hill, topped by a flower,
    a hill of bones.

They were rain-scrubbed clean,
    lovely things.
Depending how the white
    sun struck, chips of col-
or (green, yellow, dove-blue, a light
    bay) flew off the sul-
len stilled turning there. To have seen
    those clickless rings,

those prisonerless
    ribs, complex
beyond the lathe's loose jaws,
    convolute compounds
of knobs, rods, hooks, moons, absurd paws,
    subtle flats and rounds:
no man could conceive such finesse,
    concave or -vex.

Some warp like umbrella
    handles, keys
to mammoth locks. Some bend
    like equations hunting
infinity, toward which to tend.
    How it sags!—what bunting
is flesh to be hung from such ele-
    gant balconies?

YOUTH'S PROGRESS

Dick Schneider of Wisconsin . . . was elected
"Greek God" for an interfraternity ball.

—Life

When I was born, my mother taped my ears
So they lay flat. When I had aged ten years,
My teeth were firmly braced and much improved.
Two years went by; my tonsils were removed.

At fourteen, I began to comb my hair
A fancy way. Though nothing much was there,
I shaved my upper lip—next year, my chin.
At seventeen, the freckles left my skin.

Just turned nineteen, a nicely molded lad,
I said goodbye to Sis and Mother; Dad
Drove me to Wisconsin and set me loose.
At twenty-one, I was elected Zeus.

DILEMMA IN THE DELTA

An extra quarter-inch on Cleopatra's nose would
have changed the entire course of history.
                    —*Pascal, misquoted in a newspaper*

Osiris pales; the palace walls
Blush east; through slatted arches falls
The sun, who stripes the cushions where
Empires have been tucked away;
Light fills her jewels and rims her hair
And Cleopatra ripens into day.

Awake, she flings her parakeets
Some chips of cinnamon, and beats
Her scented slave, a dainty thing
Who chokes back almond tears. The queen,
Her wrist fatigued, then bids them bring
Her mirror, a mammoth aquamarine.

She rests the gem upon her thighs
And checks her features. First, the eyes:
Freight them with ink. The lips need rose
Tint: crush a rose. And something's wrong
Between her mouth and brow—her nose,
Her nose seems odd, too long. It *is* too long!

These stupid jokes of Ra! She sees,
Through veils of fury, centuries
Shifting like stirred-up camels. Men
Who wrought great deeds remain unborn,
Unthought-of heroes fight like ten,
And her own name is lost to praise or scorn.

While she lies limp, seduced by grief,
There enters, tall beyond belief,
Marc Antony, bronze-braceleted,
Conceived where Rome on Tiber sits.
Six sprigs of laurel gird his head.
His mouth is fat with avocado pits.

"Now dies," she cries, "your love, my fame!
My face shall never seem the same!"
But Marc responds, *"Deorum artis
Laudemus! Bonum hoc est omen!*
Egyptian though your cryptic heart is,
I can't resist a nose so nobly Roman."

A WOODEN DARNING EGG

The carpentered hen
unhinges her wings,
abandons her nest
of splinters, and sings.

The egg she has laid
is maple and hard
as a tenpenny nail
and smooth as a board.

The grain of the wood
embraces the shape
as brown feathers do
the rooster's round nape.

Impressured by pride,
her sandpapered throat
unwarps when she cries
Cross-cut! ka-ross-cut!

Beginning to brood
she tests with a level
the angle, sits down,
and coos *Bevel bevel.*

MR. HIGH-MIND

Then went the Jury out, whose names were **Mr.**
Blindman, Mr. *No-good*, Mr. *Malice*, Mr. *Love-*
lust, Mr. *Live-loose*, Mr. *Heady*, Mr. *High-mind*,
Mr. *Enmity*, Mr. *Lyar*, Mr. *Cruelty*, Mr. *Hate-*
light, and Mr. *Implacable*.

—*The Pilgrim's Progress*

Eleven rogues and he to judge a fool—
He files out with the jury, but distaste
Constricts his fluting nostrils, and his cool
Mind turns tepid with contempt. There is brought
A basin for him, in which to wash his hands.
Laving his palms and fingertips, he finds
An image of his white, proportioned thought
Plunged in the squalid suds of other minds.
Unmoved by Lust's requests or Hate's commands
Or Superstition's half-embarrassed bribe,
His brain takes wing and flutters up the course
First plotted by the Greeks, up toward the sphere
Where issues and alternatives are placed
In that remorseless light that knows no source.

In this banana-shaped, vanilla void,
The wise alone have cause for breathing; here
Lines parallel on earth, extended, meet.
Here priests in tweeds gyrate around the feet
Of Fact, their bride, and hymn their gratitude
That each toe of her ten is understood.
From this great height, the notion of the Good
Is seen to be a vulgar one, and crude.
High-mind as Judge descends to Earth, annoyed,
Despairing Justice. Man, a massy tribe,
Cannot possess one wide and neutral eye.
He casts his well-weighed verdict with a sigh
And for a passing moment is distressed
To see it coinciding with the rest.

THE ONE-YEAR-OLD

(After reading the appropriate chapter in *Infant
and Child in the Culture of Today*, by Arnold
Gesell and Frances Ilg)

Wakes wet; is promptly toileted;
Jargons to himself; is fed;

Executively grips a cup;
Quadrupedal, will sit up

Unaided; laughs; applauds; enjoys
Baths and manipulative toys;

Socializes (parents: shun
Excess acculturation);

Demonstrates prehension; will
Masticate yet seldom spill;

Creeps (gross motor drives are strong);
And jargons, jargons all day long.

SUPERMAN

I drive my car to supermarket,
    The way I take is superhigh,
A superlot is where I park it,
    And Super Suds are what I buy.

Supersalesmen sell me tonic—
    Super-Tone-O, for Relief.
The planes I ride are supersonic.
    In trains, I like the Super Chief.

Supercilious men and women
    Call me superficial—*me,*
Who so superbly learned to swim in
    Supercolossality.

Superphosphate-fed foods feed me;
    Superservice keeps me new.
Who would dare to supersede me,
    Super-super-superwho?

PUBLIUS VERGILIUS MARO,
THE MADISON AVENUE HICK

> This was in Italy. The year was the thirty-seventh
> before the birth of Christ. The people were
> mighty hungry, for there was a famine in the land.
> —*the beginning of a Heritage Club advertise-*
> *ment, in The New Yorker, for The Georgics*

It takes a heap o' pluggin' t' make a classic sell,
Fer folks are mighty up-to-date, an' jittery as hell;
They got no yen to set aroun' with Vergil in their laps
When they kin read the latest news in twenty-four-point
    caps.

Ye've got t' hit 'em clean an' hard, with simple predicates,
An' keep the clauses short becuz these days nobody waits
T' foller out a sentence thet all-likely lacks a punch
When in the time o' readin' they could grab a bite o' lunch.

Ye've got t' hand 'em place an' time, an' then a pinch o'
    slang
T' make 'em feel right comfy in a Latinate shebang,
An' ef your taste buds curdle an' your tum turns queasy—
    well,
It takes a heap o' pluggin' t' make a classic sell.

IN MEMORIAM

In the novel he marries Victoria but in the movie
he dies.

—caption in Life

Fate lifts us up so she can hurl
    Us down from heights of pride,
Viz.: in the book he got the girl
    But in the movie, died.

The author, seeing he was brave
    And good, rewarded him,
Then, greedy, sold him as a slave
    To savage M-G-M.

He perished on the screen, but thrives
    In print, where serifs keep
Watch o'er the happier of his lives:
    Say, Does he wake, or sleep?

PLANTING A MAILBOX

Prepare the ground when maple buds have burst
    And when the daytime moon is sliced so thin
His fibers drink blue sky with litmus thirst.
    This moment come, begin.

The site should be within an easy walk,
    Beside a road, in stony earth. Your strength
Dictates how deep you delve. The seedling's stalk
    Should show three feet of length.

Don't harrow, weed, or water; just apply
    A little gravel. Sun, and motor fumes
Perform the miracle: in late July,
    A young post office blooms.

TSOKADZE O ALTITUDO

"Tsokadze has invented a new style—apparently without knowing it. He does not bend from the waist at all. His body is straight and relaxed and leaning far out over his skis until his face is only two feet above them, his arms at his side, his head up. His bindings and shoes are so loose that only his toes touch his skies. He gets enormous distances and his flight is so beautiful."

—*Thorlief Schjelderup, quoted in the*
Times, of a young Russian ski-jumper

Tsokadze leans unknowingly
    Above his skis, relaxed and tall.
    He bends not from the waist at all.
This is the way a man should ski.

He sinks; he rises, up and up,
    His face two feet above the wood.
    This way of jumping, it is good,
Says expert Thorlief Schjelderup.

Beneath his nose, the ski-tips shake;
    He plummets down the deepening wide
    Bright pit of air, arms at his side,
His heart aloft for Russia's sake.

Loose are the bindings, taut the knees,
    Relaxed the man—see, still he flies
    And only his toes touch his skies!
Ah, c'est beau, when Tsokadze skis.

LITTLE POEMS

OVERCOME, Kim flees in bitter frustration to her TV studio dressing room where she angrily flings a vase of flowers to the floor and sobs in abandon to a rose she destroys: "I'm tearing this flower apart like I'm destroying my life." As she often does, she later turned the episode into a little poem.

—photograph caption in Life

I woke up tousled, one strap falling
    Off the shoulder, casually.
In came ten *Time-Life* lensmen, calling,
    "Novak, hold that *déshabillé!*"

I went to breakfast, asked for cocoa,
    Prunes, and toast. "Too dark," they said.
"The film we use is Pallid-Foc-O.
    Order peaches, tea, and bread."

I wrote a memo, "To my agent—"
    "Write instead," they said, " 'Dear Mum.' "
In conference, when I made a cogent
    Point, they cried, "No, no! Act dumb."

I told a rose, "I tear you as I
    Tear my life," and heard them say,
"Afraid that 'as' of yours is quasi-
    Classy. We like 'like.' O.K.?"

I dined with friends. The *Time-Life* crewmen
    Interrupted: "Bare your knees,
Project your bosom, and, for human
    Interest, look ill at ease."

I, weary, fled to bed. They hounded
    Me with meters, tripods, eyes
Of Polaroid—I was surrounded!
    The caption read, "ALONE, Kim cries."

TAO IN THE YANKEE STADIUM BLEACHERS

Distance brings proportion. From here
the populated tiers
as much as players seem part of the show:
a constructed stage beast, three folds of Dante's rose,
or a Chinese military hat
cunningly chased with bodies.
'Falling from his chariot, a drunk man is unhurt
because his soul is intact. Not knowing his fall,
he is unastonished, he is invulnerable.'
So, too, the 'pure man'—'pure'
in the sense of undisturbed water.

'It is not necessary to seek out
a wasteland, swamp, or thicket.'
The old men who saw Hans Wagner
scoop them up in lobster-hands,
the opposing pitcher's pertinent hesitations,
the sky, this meadow, Mantle's thick baked neck,
the old men who in the changing rosters see
a personal mutability,
green slats, wet stone are all to me
as when an emperor commands
a performance with a gesture of his eyes.

'No king on his throne has the joy of the dead,'
the skull told Chuang-tzu.
The thought of death is peppermint to you
when games begin with patriotic song
and a democratic sun beats broadly down.
The Inner Journey seems unjudgeably long
when small boys purchase cups of ice
and, distant as a paradise,
experts, passionate and deft,
wait while Berra flies to left.

DUE RESPECT

They [members of teen-age gangs] are respectful
of their parents and particularly of their mothers
—known as "moo" in their jargon.
                              —*New York Times Magazine*

Come moo, dear moo, let's you and me
Sit down awhile and talk togee;
My broo's at school and faa's away
A-gaaing rosebuds while he may.

Of whence we come and whii we go
Most moos nee know nor care to know,
But you are not like any oo:
You're always getting in a poo

Or working up a dreadful laa
Over nothing—nothing. Bah!
Relax. You love me, I love you,
And that's the way it shapes up, moo.

TAX-FREE ENCOUNTER

We have $3,000 savings to invest and believe in
the dignity of man. Box Y-920.
>   —*Personal notice in the Saturday Review*

I met a fellow in whose hand
Was hotly held a cool three grand.
"Inform me of," he said, "the best
Technique of gaining interest."

"Lend money at usurious rates,"
I said. "It soon accumulates."
"Oh no!" he said. "It is unsound
Artistically. Read Ezra Pound."

"Invest," I then suggested. "Deal
Yourself a hand in U.S. Steel."
He snapped, "Big businessmen are sharks.
Peruse *Das Kapital,* by Marx."

"Then buy some U.S. Savings Bonds,
For Our Defense, which corresponds
To Yours and Mine." He told me, "Cease!
Defense degrades. Read *War and Peace.*"

He added, "Dignity of men
Is what we most believe in." Then
He slyly smiled and slowly backed
Away, his principal intact.

ROOM 28

Remembered as octagonal, dark-panelled,
   And seldom frequented, except by me—
      Indeed, a bower
Attained down avenues where, framed and annalled,
   Great England's great with truculence outlive
      Their hour
And, pigmented, endure mean immortality—
   The room gave rest as some libraries give.

The visitor, approaching, brushed a girlish
   Bust of Lord Byron. James George Frazer's head,
      An unarmed sentry,
Austere, tormented, brazen-browed, and churlish,
   Guarded with sternness fit for Stygian gates
      The entry
To harmless walls where men of letters lately dead
   Were hung. The envied spot was held by Yeats.

His mask, alone a mask among the paintings,
   Attracted to itself what little sun
      The sky admitted.
Half-bronze, half-black, his Janus-face at matins
   Amazed that dim arena of the less
      Weird-witted
Survivors of a blurred time: presbyters upon
   Whose faces grieved the ghost of Earnestness.

The whites of Rider Haggard's eyes were showing
   When last I saw them. Conrad's cheeks were green,
      And Rudyard Kipling's
Pink profile burned against his brown works, glowing
   With royalties and loyal love of kings.
      Sweet stipplings

Limned the long locks that Ellen Terry, seventeen,
  Pre-Raphaelite, and blonde, let down in rings.

There Stevenson looked ill and ill-depicted;
  Frail Patmore, plucked yet gamey; Henry James,
    Our good grammarian,
More paunched and politic than I'd expected.
  Among the lone-faced portraits loomed a trin-
    Itarian
Composite: Baring, Chesterton, Belloc. The frame's
  Embellished foursquare dogma boxed them in.

Brave room! Where are they now? In college courses,
  Perused in inferior light, then laid
    On library tables.
Green knights mismounted on empirical horses,
  Encumbered by a rusty heraldry
    Of labels,
Their universe did not deserve their vows. They fade
  In pale sun, claimed by neither century.

THE SENSUALIST

Each Disc contains not more than ½ minim of
Chloroform together with Capsicum, Peppermint,
Anise, Cubeb, Licorice and Linseed.
              —*from a box of Parke-Davis throat discs*

Come, Capsicum, cast off thy membranous pods;
Thy Guinea girlhood's blossoms have been dried.
Come, Peppermint, belovèd of the gods
(That is, of Hades; Ceres, in her pride,
So Strabo says, transmogrified
Delicious Mintha, making her a plant).

Come, Anise, sweet stomachic stimulant,
Most umbelliferous of condiments,
Depart thy native haunt, the hot Levant.
Swart Licorice, or Liquorice, come hence,
And Linseed, too, of these ingredients
Most colorless, most odorless, most nil.

And Javan Cubeb, come—thy smokable
Gray pericarps and pungent seeds shall be
Our feast's incense. Come, Chloroform, née **Phyll,**
In demiminims dance unto the spree.
Compounded spices, come: dissolve in me.

SNAPSHOTS

How good of Mrs. Metz! The blur
Must be your cousin Christopher.

A scenic shot Jim took near Lyme.
Those rocks seemed lovely at the time.

And here's a product of the days
When Jim went through his gnarled tree phase.

The man behind the man in shorts—
His name is Shorer, Shaw, or Schwartz.

The kids at play. This must be Keith.
Can that be Wilma underneath?

I'd give my life to know why Josh
Sat next to Mrs. McIntosh.

Jim looked so well in checkered clothes.
I was much slimmer than this shows.

Yes, Jim and I were so in love.
That hat: what *was* I thinking of?

This disappointed Mrs. Striker.
I don't know why, it's very like her.

The dog is Skip. He loved to play.
We had to have him put away.

I guess these people are the Wrens.
There was some water on the lens.

This place is where I was inspired
To—stop me, if your eyes are tired.

MOUNTAIN IMPASSE

"I despise mountains," Stravinsky declared con-
temptuously, "they don't tell me anything."

—*Life*

Stravinsky looks upon the mountain,
    The mountain looks on him;
They look (the mountain and Stravinsky)
    And both their views are dim.

"You bore me, mountain," says Stravinsky,
    "I find you dull, and I
Despise you!" Says the mountain:
    "Stravinsky, tell me why."

Stravinsky bellows at the mountain
    And near-by valleys ring:
"You don't confide in me—Stravinsky!
    You never tell me anything!"

The hill is still before Stravinsky.
    The skies in silence glisten.
At last, a rumble, then the mountain:
    "Igor, you never listen."

A BITTER LIFE

Dr. Ycas [of the Quartermaster Research and Development Center, in a report to the National Academy of Sciences] holds that the ocean itself was alive. There were no living creatures in it.
—*New York Times*

O you Dr. Ycas you!
    In one convulsive motion
Your brain has given birth unto
    A viable young ocean.
All monsters pale beside the new:
    The Hydra, Hap, Garuda, Ra,
Italapas, Seb, Hua-hu
    Tiao, Gulltopr, Grendel's ma,
Quetzalcoatl, Kukulkan,
    Onniont, Audhumbla, Ix,
Geryon, Leviathan,
    666,
The ox Ahura Mazda made,
    The Fomors, deevs, Graiae,
And others of this ilk all fade
    Alongside Ycas' sea.
The straits were sinews, channelways
    Were veins, and islands eyes,
Rivers tails, reefs bones, and bays,
    Depending on their size,
Fists, shoulders, heads, ears, mouths, or feet;
    The fjords, as fingers, froze
Sometimes, as did the arctic pate
    And pale antarctic toes.
O horrid, horrid Ocean! The
    Foul grandmother of Tyr,
Who had nine hundred crania,
    Did not look half so queer.
It whistled with a mournful hiss

In darkness; scared and bored,
It lapped the land, yet every kiss
    Was stonily ignored.
A spheric skin, or blue-green hide,
    Alone the ocean kept
Our planet's house, yet when it died
    One aeon, no one wept.

Hap: Apis, bull-god of Egypt, reincarnation of Osiris. *Garuda:* man-bird, steed of Vishnu, Hindu. *Italapas:* coyote, one of chief Chinook Indian deities. *Seb:* otherwise Geb, Keb, or Qeb; divine goose, Egyptian. *Hua-hu Tiao:* Protean creature, snake or white rat, has the power to assume the shape of a man-eating elephant with wings, etc., Chinese. *Gulltopr:* also Goldropf; Heimdall's horse, Teutonic. *Quetzalcoatl:* name means "serpent dressed with green feathers," though he was, of course, an anthropomorphic god. Aztec. *Kukulkan:* again, feathered serpent, Maya. *Onniont:* monster snake worshiped by Huron Indians. *Audhumbla:* cow who nourished Ymir, the first giant; both sprang from the mist, Norse. *Ix:* one of the four Bacabs, who stood at the four corners of the world and held it up, Maya. *Geryon:* three heads, three bodies, enormous wings, son of Chrysaor and Cillirrhoe, lived on Erythia, Greek. *666:* beast of Revelation 13. *The ox Ahura Mazda made:* a raging, senseless creature; the first creative effort in the animal line made by the Persian Lord of Wisdom. *Fomors:* hideous misshapen monsters representing the kingdom of darkness, Celtic. *deevs:* Persian evil spirits, huge and ugly; long horns, tails, and fangs. *Graiae:* gray-haired women, had only one tooth among them, Greek.

GLASSES

I wear them. They help me. But I
Don't care for them. Two birds, steel hinges
Haunt each an edge of the small sky
My green eyes make. Rim-horn impinges
Upon my vision's furry fringes;
Faint dust collects upon the dry,
Unblinking shield behind which cringes
My naked, deprecated eye.

My gaze feels aimed. It is as if
Two manufactured beams had been
Lodged in my sockets—hollow, stiff,
And gray, like mailing tubes—and when
I pivot, vases topple down
From tabletops, and women frown.

A RACK OF PAPERBACKS

Gateway, Grove,
   and Dover say,
"Unamuno
   any day."

Beacon Press
   and Torchlight chorus,
"Kierkegaard
   does nicely for us."

"Willey, Waley,"
   Anchor bleats,
"Auden, Barzun,
   Kazin, Keats."

"Tovey, Glover,
   Cohen, Fry"
is Meridi-
   an's reply.

"Bentley's best,"
   brags Dramabooks.
Harvest burgeons
   Cleanth Brooks.

All, including
   Sentinel,
Jaico, Maco,
   Arco, Dell,

Noonday, Vintage,
   Living Age,
Mentor, Wisdom—
   page on page

of classics much
   too little known
when books were big
   and bindings sewn—

agree: "Lord Raglan,
   Margaret Mead,
Moses Hadas,
   Herbert Read,

the Panchatantra,
   Hamsun's 'Pan,'
Tillich, Ilg,
   Kahlil Gibran,

and Henry James
   sell better if
their spines are not
   austerely stiff."

POPULAR REVIVALS, 1956

The thylacine, long thought to be extinct,
Is not. The ancient dog-like creature, linked
To kangaroos and platypi, still pounces
On his Tasmanian prey, the *Times* announces.

The tarpan (stumpy, prehistoric horse)
Has been rebred—in Germany, of course.
Herr Heinz Heck, by striking genetic chords,
Has out of plowmares beat his tiny wards.

The California fur seal, a refined
And gullible amphibian consigned
By profit-seeking sealers to perdition,
Barked at the recent Gilmore expedition.

The bison, butchered on our Western prairie,
Took refuge in our coinage. Now, contrary
To what was feared, the herds are out of danger
And in the films, co-starred with Stewart Granger.

ODE III.ii : HORACE

Let the boy, timber-tough from vigorous soldiering,
learn to endure lack amicably,
and let him, horseman feared for his javelin,
plague the ferocious men of Parthos;

let him live his life lower than heaven
in the midst of restless things. Seeing him
from enemy ramparts, may the warring tyrant's wife
and the young ripe woman breathe, "Ah,

let not our kingly lover, clumsy
in the swirl of combat, stroke the lion
rough-to-the-touch, whom fury for blood
thrusts through the thick of the slaughter!"

Sweet it is, and seemly, to die for country.
Death overtakes the runaway as well,
and does not spare the coward backs
and knees of youths who are not warlike.

Manliness, not knowing the taint of defeat,
flashes forth with unsullied glory,
neither lifts nor lowers the axes
at a whisper from the scatterbrained mob.

Manliness, that throws open heaven to those
undeserving of death, plots its course
by a route denied to most, and on pinion
soaring scorns the common crowd, the damp earth.

There is, for faithful silence, too,
sure reward. I will forbid the man who spreads abroad
occult Ceres' sacred rites
to exist beneath a roof or to unmoor a frail craft

with me. Often slighted Jupiter
involves the unpolluted with the impure;
rarely does Poena not catch the wicked man,
though he has the head start, and her step is hesitant.

A CHEERFUL ALPHABET OF
PLEASANT OBJECTS
to David

APPLE

Since Time began, such alphabets begin
With Apple, source of Knowledge and of Sin.
My child, take heart: the fruit that undid Man
Brought out as well the best in Paul Cézanne.

BIRDBATH

The birdbath is a placid eye
Beneath the apple trees; the sky
Is by the birdbath seldom seen,
And hence its water is brown-green.

When blackbirds come to purge their wings,
The water darkens; one wren brings
A touch of rust; the oriole
Casts down a casual aureole.

Trees ripen; then the birdbath glows
With dimpled hints of gold and rose.
Leaves fall, and thus unveil the sky;
But now the birdbath is bone dry.

COG

No, not for him the darkly planned
    Ambiguities of flesh.
His maker gave him one command:
    Mesh.

DOILY

Along the upland meadows
    of the dining-table bloom
the doilies, openfaced and
    white; within the living-room
they cling to every slope of
    chair, and pattern each plateau.
Around the trunks of lamps whose
    shades exude a healthy glow,
the doily spreads her petals
    made of ivory and cream.
Hands off! Who plucks a doily
    bothers Nature's farflung Scheme.

EASY CHAIR

Avoid the clicking three-way lamp; beware
   The throw rug's coils, the two-faced sofabed,
   The vile lowboy; but more than any, dread
The hippopotomastic easy chair.

For, seated, you shall sink and never rise.
   The slow osmosis of the chair's embrace
   Shall make your arms *its* arms, and make your face
An antimacassar monogrammed with eyes.

FLOWERPOT	GERANIUM
This clayey fez,	Who has this home?
inverted, is	Geranium,
a shoe for roots:	a maiden plant
an orange boot	and aspirant
wherein one leg	to broader green.
goes down to beg	Against the screen
more dirt. Alas,	she leans her head,
in vain it asks.	inhibited.

More Dirt (the moral runs) or Else We Wane—
See D. H. Lawrence, Ovid, or Mark Twain.

HAIRBRUSH

Made of hair,
it brushes locks
of hair:
       and there,
my son,
you have a Chinese paradox,
but not much of one.

ICEBOX

In Daddy's day there were such things:
    Wood cabinets of cool
In which a cake of ice was placed
    While he was off at school.

Blue-veined, partitioned in itself,
    The cake seemed cut of air
Which had exploded; one cracked star
    Appeared imprisoned there.

The corners wore throughout the day;
    The slats whereon it rested
Seeped upwards, so the slippery base
    Became severely crested.

Eventually an egg so small
    It could be tossed away,
The ice cake vanished quite, as has
    That rather distant day.

JACK

A card, a toy, a hoist,
a flag, a stay, a fruit,
a sailor, John, a pot,
a rabbit, knife, and boot;
o'-lantern, in-the-box
or -pulpit, Ketch, a daw,
a-dandy, of-all-trades,
anapes, an ass, a straw.

KNOB

Conceptually a blob,
the knob
is a smallish object which,
hitched
to a larger,
acts as verger.

It enables
us to gain access to drawers in end tables;
it shepherds
us into cupboards.

LETTER SLOT

Once each day this broad mouth spews

Apologies,

bills,

rags,

and news.

MIRROR

When you look   kool uoy nehW
into a mirror   rorrim a otni
it is not   ton si ti
yourself you see,   ,ees uoy flesruoy
but a kind   dnik a tub
of apish error   rorre hsipa fo
posed in fearful   lufraef ni desop
symmetry.   .yrtemmys

NUTCRACKER

His teeth are part of his shoulders because
A **nut**
Is broken best by arms that serve as jaws.

OTTOMAN

Lessons in history: the Greeks
Were once more civilized than Swedes.
Iranians were, for several weeks,
     Invincible, as Medes.

The mild Mongolians, on a spree,
Beheaded half of Asia; and
The Arabs, in their century,
     Subdued a world of sand.

Just so, the cushioned stool we deign
To sit on, called the Ottoman:
We would not dare, were this the reign
     Of Sultan Selim Khan.

From India to Hungary
The Ottoman held sway; his scope
Extended well into the sea
     And terrified the Pope.

And Bulgar, Mameluke, and Moor
All hastened to kowtow
To tasseled bits of furniture.
     It seems fantastic now.

PENDULUM

This lean commuter busies
Himself with being steady;
No matter where he is, he's
Been often there already.

QUILT

The quilt that covers all of us, to date,
Has patches numbered 1 to 48,*
Five northern rents, a crooked central seam,
   A ragged eastern edge, a way
   Of bunching uglily, and a
Perhaps too energetic color scheme.

Though shaken every twenty years, this fine
Old quilt was never beaten on the line.
It took long making. Generations passed
   While thread was sought, and calico
   And silk were coaxed from Mexico
And France. The biggest squares were added last.

Don't kick your covers, son. The bed is built
So you can never shake the clinging quilt
That blanketed your birth and tries to keep
   Your waking warm, impalpable
   As atmosphere. As earth it shall
Be tucked about you through your longest sleep.

* Since I composed this rather nifty
  Couplet, the number rose to 50.

91

RAINSPOUT

Up the house's nether corner,
Snaky-skilled, the burglar shinnies,
Peeking, cautious, in the dormer,
Creeping, wary, where the tin is.

Stealthily he starts to burgle.
Hear his underhanded mutter;
Hear him, with a guilty gurgle,
Pour his loot into the gutter.

STOPPER

Take instead the honest stopper,
Crying "halt" to running water,
Chained to duty, as is proper
For a piece of rubber mortar.

Dense resistance is the *raison
D'être* of this dull sentry; certes
He shall hold the brimming basin
Even after water dirties.

TRIVET

"What is it? Why?" Thus the trivet,
   Like a piece of algebra,
Embraces mysteries which give it
   Quelque chose, je ne sais quoi.

UMBRELLA

Unfurl it when the heavens burst,
    And hold it over ladies.
Observe taboos; the thing, accurst,
    Was hatched in humid Hades.

Don't treat it as a cane. Don't poke
    The end at friends; you're liable
To give offense. Don't stick a spoke
    In anybody's eyeball.

Vacuum cleaner

This baggy broom,
whose hum is doom,
refutes for the obtuse
the thought that Nothing has no use:
no, nothing better tidies up a mess
than Nothingness.

WHEEL

For all of his undoubted skill
The Inca lacked the wheel until
Pizarro came to high Peru
And said that llamas wouldn't do.

The Eskimos had never heard
Of centripetal force when Byrd
Bicycled up onto a floe
And told them, "This how white man go."

Nepal's Joe Averageperson feels
He should get by on prayer wheels.
The Navajos retread their squaws.
So lucky, lucky you, because

Whereas, below the pyramids
In Africa, some hominids
Have waited since the Pliocene,
You'll get the wheel at age sixteen.

XYSTER

"An instrument for scraping bones"
Defines the knife.
The word is rarely used—but why?
What else is life?

Yardstick

Like Milton's measuring the twofold world
in constantly decasyllabic pentameters,
the yardstick trims the epic of land and air
and has it trip obsequiously to trimeters,
each foot made of just twelve symbols each.

ZEPPELIN

A German specialty, since men
    Of other nations must inveigle
Helium or hydrogen;
    But Germany had Hegel.

It fell, as do Philosophy's
    Symmetric, portly darlings,
Fell down from skies where one still sees
    Religion's narrow starlings.

TELEPHONE POLES
and other poems

(1963)

TO E. B. AND K. S. WHITE

*in gratitude for good example
and kind counsel*

I

BENDIX

This porthole overlooks a sea
Forever falling from the sky,
The water inextricably
Involved with buttons, suds, and dye.

Like bits of shrapnel, shards of foam
Fly heavenward; a bedsheet heaves,
A stocking wrestles with a comb,
And cotton angels wave their sleeves.

The boiling purgatorial tide
Revolves our dreary shorts and slips,
While Mother coolly bakes beside
Her little jugged apocalypse.

REEL

whorl (hwûrl; hwôrl), *n.* . . . 2. Something that
whirls or seems to whirl as a whorl, or wharve . . .
         —Webster's Collegiate Dictionary

Whirl, whorl or wharve! The world
Whirls within solar rings
Which once were hotly hurled
Away by whirling things!

Wind whirls; hair curls; the worm
Can turn, and wheels can wheel,
And even stars affirm:
Whatever whirls is real.

We whirl, or seem to whirl,
Or seem to seem to; whorls
Within more whorls unfurl
In matters, habits, morals.

And when we go and carve
An onion or a tree,
We find, within, a wharve
And, in the wharve, a whee!

COSMIC GALL

Every second, hundreds of billions of these neutrinos pass through each square inch of our bodies, coming from above during the day and from below at night, when the sun is shining on the other side of the earth!

—From "An Explanatory Statement on Elementary Particle Physics," by M. A. Ruderman and A. H. Rosenfeld, in American Scientist.

Neutrinos, they are very small.
    They have no charge and have no mass
And do not interact at all.
The earth is just a silly ball
    To them, through which they simply pass,
Like dustmaids down a drafty hall
    Or photons through a sheet of glass.
    They snub the most exquisite gas,
Ignore the most substantial wall,
    Cold-shoulder steel and sounding brass,
Insult the stallion in his stall,
    And, scoring barriers of class,
Infiltrate you and me! Like tall
And painless guillotines, they fall
    Down through our heads into the grass.
At night, they enter at Nepal
    And pierce the lover and his lass
From underneath the bed—you call
    It wonderful: I call it crass.

I have now worn the same terylene tie every day
for eighteen months.
> —*From "Chemistry," a Penguin book by*
> *Kenneth Hutton*

My tie is made of terylene;
   Eternally I wear it,
For time can never wither, stale,
   Shred, shrink, fray, fade, or tear it.
The storms of January fail
   To loosen it with bluster;
The rains of April fail to stain
   Its polyester lustre;
July's hot sun beats down in vain;
   October's frosts fall futilely;
December's snow can blow and blow—
   My tie remains acutely
Immutable! When I'm below,
   Dissolving in that halcyon
Retort, my carbohydrates shed
   From off my frame of calcium—
When I am, in lay language, dead,
   Across my crumbling sternum
Shall lie a spanking fresh cravat
   Unsullied *ad æternum,*
A grave and solemn prospect that
   Makes light of our allotted
Three score and ten, for terylene
   Shall never be unknotted.

THE DESCENT OF MR. ALDEZ

Mr. Aldez, a cloud physicist, came down last year
to study airborne ice crystals.
—Dispatch from Antarctica in the Times

That cloud—ambiguous, not
a horse, or a whale, but what?—
comes down through the crystalline mist.
It is a physicist!

Like fog, on cat's feet, tiptoeing
to where the bits of ice are blowing,
it drifts, and eddies, and spies
its prey through vaporous eyes

and pounces! With billowing paws
the vague thing smokily claws
the fluttering air, notes its traits,
smiles knowingly, and dissipates.

CALIGULA'S DREAM

Insomnia was his worst torment. Three hours a
night of fitful sleep was all that he ever got, and
even then terrifying visions would haunt him—
once, for instance, he dreamed that he had a conversation with the Mediterranean Sea.

—*Suetonius*

Of gold the bread on which he banqueted,
Where pimps in silk and pearls dissolved in wine
Were standard fare. The monster's marble head
Had many antic veins, being divine.
At war, he massed his men upon the beach
And bawled the coward's order, "Gather shells!"
And stooped, in need of prisoners, to teach
The German tongue to prostituted Gauls.
Bald young, broad-browed and, for his era, tall,
In peace he proved incestuous and queer,
And spent long hours in the Capitol
Exchanging compliments with Jupiter;
He stalled his horse in ivory, and displayed
His wife undressed to friends, and liked to view
Eviscerations and the dance, and made
Poor whores supply imperial revenue.

Perhaps—to plead—the boy had heard how when
They took his noble father from the pyre
And found a section unconsumed, the men
Suspicioned: "Poisoned hearts resist the fire."
It was as water that his vision came,
At any rate—more murderous than he,
More wanton, uglier, of wider fame,
Unsleeping also, multi-sexed, the Sea.

It told him, "Little Boots, you cannot sin
Enough; you speak a language, though you rave.
The actual things at home beneath my skin

108

Out-horrify the vilest hopes you have.
Ten-tentacled invertebrates embrace
And swap through thirsty ana livid seed
While craggy worms without a brain or face
Upon their own soft children blindly feed.
As huge as Persian palaces, blue whales
Grin fathoms down, and through their teeth are strained
A million lives a minute; each entails,
In death, a microscopic bit of pain.
Atrocity is truly emperor;
All things that thrive are slaves of cruel Creation."

Caligula, his mouth a mass of fur,
Awoke, and toppled toward assassination.

WHITE DWARF

Discovery of the smallest known star in the universe was announced today . . . The star is about
one half the diameter of the moon.

—The Times

Welcome, welcome, little star!
I'm delighted that you are
Up in Heaven's vast extent,
No bigger than a continent.

Relatively minuscule,
Spinning like a penny spool,
Glinting like a polished spoon,
A kind of kindled demi-moon,

You offer cheer to tiny Man
'Mid galaxies Gargantuan—
A little pill in endless night,
An antidote to cosmic fright.

TOOTHACHE MAN

The earth has been unkind to him.
    He lies in middle strata.
The time capsules about him brim
    With advertising matter.

His addled fossils tell a tale
    That lacks barbaric splendor;
His vertebrae are small and pale,
    His femora are slender.

It is his teeth—strange, cratered things—
    That name him. Some are hollow,
Like bowls, and hold gold offerings.
    The god may be Apollo.

Silver and gold. We think he thought
    His god, who was immortal,
Dwelt in his skull; hence, the devout
    Adorned the temple's portal.

Heraldic fists and spears and bells
    In all metallic colors
Invade the bone; their volume swells
    On backward through the molars.

This culture's meagre sediments
    Have come to light just lately.
We handle them with reverence.
    He must have suffered greatly.

DEITIES AND BEASTS

Tall Atlas, Jupiter, Hercules, Thor,
Just like the antic pagan gods of yore,
Make up a too-erratic pantheon
For mortal men to be dependent on.

I much prefer, myself, the humble RAT,
The tiny Terrier, the short Hawk that
Makes secret flight, and the Sparrow, whose fall
Is never mentioned in the press at all.

SONIC BOOM

I'm sitting in the living room,
When, up above, the Thump of Doom
Resounds. Relax. It's sonic boom.

The ceiling shudders at the clap,
The mirrors tilt, the rafters snap,
And Baby wakens from his nap.

"Hush, babe. Some pilot we equip,
Giving the speed of sound the slip,
Has cracked the air like a penny whip."

Our world is far from frightening; I
No longer strain to read the sky
Where moving fingers (jet planes) fly.
Our world seems much too tame to die.

And if it does, with one more *pop*,
I shan't look up to see it drop.

PARTY KNEE

To drink in moderation, and to smoke
   A minimal amount, and joke
   Reservedly does not insure
Awaking from a party whole and pure.

Be we as temperate as the turtledove,
   A soiree is an orgy of
   This strange excess, unknown in France,
And Rome, and Nineveh: the upright stance.

When more than four forgather in our land,
   We stand, and stand, and stand, and stand;
   Thighs ache, and drowsy numbness locks
The bones between our pockets and our socks.

Forgive us, Prince of Easement, when from **bed**
   With addled knees and lucid head
   We leap at dawn, and sob, and beg
A buffered aspirin for a splitting leg.

THOUGHTS
WHILE DRIVING HOME

Was I clever enough? Was I charming?
Did I make at least one good pun?
Was I disconcerting? Disarming?
Was I wise? Was I wan? Was I fun?

Did I answer that girl with white shoulders
Correctly, or should I have said
(Engagingly), "Kierkegaard smolders,
But Eliot's ashes are dead"?

And did I, while being a smarty,
Yet some wry reserve slyly keep,
So they murmured, when I'd left the party,
"He's deep. He's deep. He's deep"?

IDYLL

Within a quad of aging brick,
Behind the warty warden oak,
The Radcliffe sophomores exchange,
In fencing costume, stroke for stroke;
Their bare knees bent, the darlings duel
Like daughters of Dumas and Scott.
Their sneakered feet torment the lawn,
Their skirted derrières stick out.

Beneath the branches, needles glint
Unevenly in dappled sun
As shadowplay and swordplay are
In no time knitted into one;
The metal twitters, girl hacks girl,
Their educated faces caged.
The fake felt hearts and pointless foils
Contain an oddly actual rage.

A SONG OF PATERNAL CARE

A Lithuanian lithographer
   Who lived on lithia water
Was blessed, by lithogenesis,
   With a lithe and lithic daughter.

Said he beneath a lithy tree
   When she'd reached litholysis,
"It's time you thought of lithomarge,
   And even . . . lithophthisis."

She blushed, the lovely lithoglyph,
   And said, "I love a lithsman.*
I feel so litholyte when I'm,"
   She smiled, eliding, "wi' th's man."

"Go fetch the lithofellic fellow!"
   Her father boomed, with laughter.
She did. They lived in Lithgow, Aus.,
   Litherly** ever after.

* An unfortunately obsolete word meaning a sailor in the navy under the Danish kings of England.
** Another, meaning mischievous, wicked, or lazy.

MARRIAGE COUNSEL

WHY MARRY OGRE
JUST TO GET HUBBY?
—*Headline in the Boston Herald*

Why marry ogre
    Just to get hubby?
Has he a brogue, or
    Are his legs stubby?

Smokes he a stogie?
    Is he not sober?
Is he too logy
    And dull as a crowbar?

Tom, Dick, and Harry:
    Garrulous, greedy,
And grouchy. They vary
    From savage to seedy,

And, once wed, will parry
    To be set asunder.
O harpy, why marry
    Ogre? I wonder.

RECITAL

ROGER BOBO GIVES
RECITAL ON TUBA
—*Headline in the Times*

Eskimos in Manitoba,
   Barracuda off Aruba,
Cock an ear when Roger Bobo
   Starts to solo on the tuba.

Men of every station—Pooh-Bah,
   Nabob, bozo, toff, and hobo—
Cry in unison, "Indubi-
   Tably, there is simply nobo-

Dy who oompahs on the tubo,
Solo, quite like Roger Bubo!"

TROPICAL BEETLES

Composed of horny, jagged blacks
    Yet quite unformidable,
They flip themselves upon their backs
    And die beneath the table.

The Temperate wasp, with pointed moan,
    Flies straightway to the apple;
But bugs inside the Tropic Zone
    With idle fancies grapple.

They hurl themselves past window sills
    And labor through a hundred
Ecstatic, crackling, whirring spills—
    For what, I've often wondered.

They seek the light—it stirs their stark,
    Ill-lit imaginations—
And win, when stepped on in the dark,
    Disgusted exclamations.

B. W. I.

Under a priceless sun,
  Shanties and guava.
Beside an emerald sea,
  Lumps of lava.

On the white dirt road,
  A blind man tapping.
On dark Edwardian sofas,
  White men napping.

In half-caste twilight, heartfelt
  Songs to Jesus.
Across the arid land,
  Ocean breezes.
The sibilance of sadness
  Never ceases.

The empty cistern.
  The broken Victrola.
The rusted praise of
  Coca-Cola.

Old yellow tablecloths,
  And tea, and hairy
Goats, and airmail
  Stationery.

Copies of *Punch* and *Ebony*.
  Few flowers.
Just the many-petalled sun above
  The endless hours.

EXPOSURE

Please do not tell me there is no voodoo,
For, if so, how then do you
Explain that a photograph of a head
Always tells if the person is living or dead?

Always. I have never known it to fail.
There is something misted in the eyes, something pale,
If not in the lips, then in the hair—
It is hard to put your finger on, but there.

A kind of third dimension settles in:
A blur, a kiss of otherness, a milky film.
If, while you hold a snapshot of Aunt Flo,
Her real heart stops, you will know.

COMP. RELIGION

It all begins with fear of *mana*.
  Next there comes the love of tribe.
Native dances, totems, ani-
  Mism and magicians thrive.

Culture grows more complicated.
  Spirits, chiefs in funny hats,
And suchlike spooks are sublimated
  Into gods and ziggurats.

Polyarmed and polyheaded,
  Gods proliferate until
Puristic-minded sages edit
  Their welter into one sweet Will.

This worshipped One grows so enlightened,
  Vast, and high He, in a blur,
Explodes; and men are left as frightened
  Of *mana* as they ever were.

BESTIARY

If the transmigration of a soul takes place into a rational being, it simply becomes the soul of that body. But if the soul migrates into a brute beast, it follows the body outside as a guardian spirit follows a man.

—Sallustius

Each bird is chased by another bird,
　　Each worm by a shadow worm,
Much as each thing has a word
　　Guarding its spirit and form.

These are the rational souls;
　　Unable to enter, they float
Behind the brutes, the fishes and fowls,
　　As a dory is dragged by a boat.

This accounts for the animal world—
　　Its qualms and skittering fears—
For each squirrel feels a rational squirrel
　　Pressing on its ears.

THE HIGH-HEARTS

Assumption of erect posture in man lifts the heart
higher above the ground than in any other animal
now living except the giraffe and the elephant.
  —*From an article titled "Anatomy" in the
  Encyclopaedia Britannica*

Proud elephant, by accident of bulk,
Upreared the mammoth cardiacal hulk
That plunged his storm of blood through canvas veins.
Enthroned beneath his tusks, unseen, it reigns
In dark state, stoutly ribbed, suffused with doubt,
Where lions have to leap to seek it out.

Herbivorous giraffe, in dappled love
With green and sunstruck edibles above,
Yearned with his bones; in an aeon or so,
His glad heart left his ankles far below,
And there, where forelegs turn to throat, it trem-
Bles like a blossom halfway up a stem.

Poor man, an ape, anxious to use his paws,
Became erect and held the pose because
His brain, developing beyond his ken,
Kept whispering, "The universe wants men."
So still he strains to keep his heart aloft,
Too high and low at once, too hard and soft.

THE MENAGERIE
AT VERSAILLES IN 1775

Taken verbatim from a notebook kept by
Dr. Samuel Johnson

Cygnets dark; their black feet;
on the ground; tame.
Halcyons, or gulls.
Stag and hind, small.
Aviary, very large: the net, wire.
Black stag of China, small.

Rhinoceros, the horn broken
and pared away, which, I suppose,
will grow; the basis, I think,
four inches 'cross; the skin
folds like loose cloth doubled over his body
and 'cross his hips: a vast animal,
though young; as big, perhaps,
as four oxen.

           The young elephant,
with his tusks just appearing.
The brown bear put out his paws.
All very tame. The lion.
The tigers I did not well view.
The camel, or dromedary with two bunches
called the Huguin, taller than any horse.
Two camels with one bunch.

Among the birds was a pelican,
who being let out, went
to a fountain, and swam
about to catch fish. His feet
well webbed: he dipped his head,
and turned his long bill sidewise.

This passage may be found, in prose and punctuated a bit differently,
on pp. 555-6 of the Modern Library Giant edition of Boswell's *Life*.

UPON LEARNING THAT
A BIRD EXISTS
CALLED THE TURNSTONE

A turnstone turned rover
And went through ten turnstiles,
Admiring the clover
And turnsole and fern styles.

The Turneresque landscape
She scanned for a lover;
She'd heard one good turnstone
Deserves another.

She took to the turnpike
And travelled to Dover,
Where turnips enjoy
A rapid turnover.

In vain did she hover
And earnestly burn
With yearning; above her
The terns cried, "Return!"

UPON LEARNING THAT
A TOWN EXISTS IN VIRGINIA
CALLED UPPERVILLE

In Upperville, the upper crust
Say "Bottoms up!" from dawn to dusk
And "Ups-a-daisy, dear!" at will—
I want to live in Upperville.

One-upmanship is there the rule,
And children learn about, at school,
"The Rise of Silas Lapham" and
Why gravitation has been banned.

High hamlet, ho!—my mind's eye sees
Thy ruddy uplands, lofty trees,
Upsurging streams, and towering dogs;
There are no valleys, dumps, or bogs.

Depression never dares intrude
Upon thy sweet upswinging mood;
Downcast, long-fallen, let me go
To where the cattle never low.

I've always known there was a town
Just right for me; I'll settle down
And be uplifted all day long—
Fair Upperville, accept my song.

ZULUS LIVE IN LAND
WITHOUT A SQUARE

A Zulu lives in a round world. If he does not leave
his reserve, he can live his whole life through and
never see a straight line.
> *—Headline and text from the Times*

In Zululand the huts are round,
The windows oval, and the rooves
Thatched parabolically. The ground
Is tilled in curvilinear grooves.

When Zulus cannot smile, they frown,
To keep an arc before the eye.
Describing distances to town,
They say, "As flies the butterfly."

Anfractuosity is king.
Melodic line itself is banned,
Though all are hep enough to sing—
There are no squares in Zululand.

POP SMASH, OUT OF
ECHO CHAMBER

O truly, Lily was a lulu,
  Doll, and dilly of a belle;
No one's smile was more enamelled,
No one's style was more untrammelled,
  Yet her records failed to sell
      Well.

Her agent, Daley, duly worried,
  Fretted, fidgeted, complained,
Daily grew so somber clever
Wits at parties said whenever
  Lily waxed, poor Daley waned.
      Strained

Beyond endurance, feeling either
  He or Lily must be drowned,
Daley, dulled to Lily's lustre,
Deeply down a well did thrust her.
  Lily yelled; he dug the sound,
      Found

A phone, contacted Victor,
  Cut four sides; they sold, and how!
Daley disclaims credit; still, he
Likes the lucre. As for Lily,
  She is dry and famous now.
      Wow.

THE MODERATE

Frost's space is deeper than Poliakoff's and not as
deep as that of Soulages.
                                        —*Patrick Heron in Arts*

"Soulages's space is deep and wide—
Beware!" they said. "Beware," they cried,
"The yawning gap, the black abyss
That closes with a dreadful hiss!

"That shallow space by Poliakoff,"
They added, "is a wretched trough.
It wrinkles, splinters, shreds, and fades;
It wouldn't hold the Jack of Spades."

"But where?" I asked, bewildered, lost.
"Go seek," they said, "the space of Frost;
It's not too bonny, not too braw—
The nicest space you ever saw."

I harked, and heard, and here I live,
Delighted to be relative.

KENNETHS

Rextroth and Patchen and Fearing—their mothers
Perhaps could distinguish their sons from the others,
But I am unable. My inner eye pictures
A three-bodied sun-lover issuing strictures,
Berating "Tom" Eliot, translating tanka,
Imbibing espresso and sneering at Sanka—
Six arms, thirty fingers, all writing abundantly
What pops into heads each named Kenneth, redundantly.

TOME-THOUGHTS,
FROM THE TIMES

The special merit of the two first novels up for
discussion today is that they are neither overly
ambitious nor overly long. Both are deftly written,
amusing and intensely feminine. Both are the work
of brightly talented young women.

> —*Orville Prescott, in The New York Times*

Oh, to be Orville Prescott
Now that summer's here,
And the books on tinted paper
Blow lightly down the air,
And the merciful brevity of every page
Becalms the winter's voluminous rage,
And unambition like lilac lies
On Prescott's eyes.

When heroines with small frustrations,
Dressed in transparent motivations,
Glimmer and gambol, trip and trot;
Then may the sensitive critic spy,
Beneath the weave of a gossamer plot,
The subtle pink of an author's thigh.
Oh bliss! oh brightly talented! oh neither
Overly this nor that—a breather!
Along the sands of the summer lists
The feminine first novelists
Go dancing, deft, and blessed twice over
By Prescott, deep in short-stemmed clover.

I MISSED HIS BOOK,
BUT I READ HIS NAME

"The Silver Pilgrimage," by M. Anantanarayanan.
... 160 pages. Criterion. $3.95.

—The Times

Though authors are a dreadful clan
To be avoided if you can,
I'd like to meet the Indian,
M. Anantanarayanan.

I picture him as short and tan.
We'd meet, perhaps, in Hindustan.
I'd say, with admirable *élan*,
"Ah, Anantanarayanan—

I've heard of you. The *Times* once ran
A notice on your novel, an
Unusual tale of God and Man."
And Anantanarayanan

Would seat me on a lush divan
And read his name—that sumptuous span
Of "a's" and "n's" more lovely than
"In Xanadu did Kubla Khan"—

Aloud to me all day. I plan
Henceforth to be an ardent fan
Of Anantanarayanan—
M. Anantanarayanan.

AGATHA CHRISTIE
AND BEATRIX POTTER

Many-volumed authoresses
In capacious country dresses,
Full of cheerful art and nearly
Perfect craft, we love you dearly.

You know the hedgerow, stile, and barrow,
Have sniffed the cabbage, leek, and marrow,
Have heard the prim postmistress snicker,
And spied out murder in the vicar.

You've drawn the berry-beaded brambles
Where Mrs. Tiggy-Winkle rambles,
And mapped the attics in the village
Where mice plot alibis and pillage.

God bless you, girls, for in these places
You give us cozy scares and chases
That end with innocence acquitted—
Except for Cotton-tail, who did it.

MEDITATION ON A NEWS ITEM

Fidel Castro, who considers himself first in war
and first in peace, was first in the Hemingway
fishing tourney at Havana, Cuba. "I am a novice
at fishing," said Fidel. "You are a lucky novice,"
replied Ernest.

—*Life, in June, 1960*

Yes, yes, and there is even a photograph,
of the two in profile, both bearded, both sharp-nosed,
both (though the one is not wearing a cap
and the other is not carrying a cat)
magnificently recognizable (do
you think that much-photographed faces grow
larger, more deeply themselves, like flowers
in sunlight?). A great cup sits between their chests.

Life does not seem to think it very strange.
It runs the shot cropped to four inches,
and the explanation is given in full above.
But to me it seems immeasurably strange: as strange
to me as if there were found,
in a Jacobean archive, an unquestionably authentic
woodcut showing Shakespeare
presenting the blue ribbon for Best Cake Baked
to Queen Elizabeth.

And even the dialogue: so perfect—
"You are a lucky novice." Succinct,
wry, ominous, innocent: Nick Adams talking.
How did it happen? Did he,
convulsively departing from the exhausting regimen—
the rising at 6 a.m. to sharpen twelve pencils
with which to cut, as he stands at his bookcase,
269 or 312 or 451 more words into the paper
that will compose one of those many rumored books
that somehow never appear—did he abruptly exclaim,

"I must have a fishing tourney!"
and have posters painted and posted
in cabañas, cigar stores, and bordellos,
ERNEST HEMINGWAY FISHING COMPETITION,
just like that?

And did he receive, on one of those soft Havana mornings,
while the smoky-green Caribbean laps the wharf legs,
and the *señoritas* yawn behind grillwork,
and the black mailmen walk in khaki shorts,
an application blank stating CASTRO, Fidel?
Occupation: Dictator. *Address:*
Top Floor, Habana-Hilton Hotel (commandeered).
Hobbies: Ranting, U.S.-Baiting, Fishing (novice).

And was it honest? I mean, did Castro
wade down off the beach in hip boots
in a long cursing line of other contestants, Cubans,
cabdrivers, pimps, restaurant waiters, small landowners,
and make his cast, the bobbin singing,
and the great fish leap, with a splash
leap from the smoky-green waves,
and he, tugging, writhing, bring it in
and stand there, mopping the brow
of his somehow fragile, Apollonian profile
while the great man panted back and forth
plying his tape measure?

And at the award ceremony,
did their two so-different sorts of fame—
yet tangent on the point of beards and love of exploit—
create in the air one of those eccentric electronic disturb-
          ances
to which our younger physicists devote so much thought?
In the photograph, there is some sign of it:

137

they seem beatified, and resemble
two apostles by Dürer, possibly Peter and Paul.

My mind sinks down through the layers of strangeness:
I am as happy as if I had opened
a copy of "Alice in Wonderland"
in which the heroine *does* win the croquet contest
administered by the Queen of Hearts.

II

TELEPHONE POLES

They have been with us a long time.
They will outlast the elms.
Our eyes, like the eyes of a savage sieving the trees
In his search for game,
Run through them. They blend along small-town streets
Like a race of giants that have faded into mere mythology.
Our eyes, washed clean of belief,
Lift incredulous to their fearsome crowns of bolts, trusses,
       struts, nuts, insulators, and such
Barnacles as compose
These weathered encrustations of electrical debris—
Each a Gorgon's head, which, seized right,
Could stun us to stone.

Yet they are ours. We made them.
See here, where the cleats of linemen
Have roughened a second bark
Onto the bald trunk. And these spikes
Have been driven sideways at intervals handy for human
      legs.
The Nature of our construction is in every way
A better fit than the Nature it displaces.
What other tree can you climb where the birds' twitter,
Unscrambled, is English? True, their thin shade is
      negligible,
But then again there is not that tragic autumnal
Casting-off of leaves to outface annually.
These giants are more constant than evergreens
By being never green.

WASH

For seven days it rained that June;
A storm half out to sea kept turning around like a dog
      trying to settle himself on a rug;
We were the fleas that complained in his hair.

On the eighth day, before I had risen,
My neighbors' clothes had rushed into all the back yards
And lifted up their arms in praise.

From an upstairs window it seemed prehistorical:
Through the sheds and fences and vegetable gardens,
Workshirts and nightgowns, long-soaked in the cellar,

Underpants, striped towels, diapers, child's overalls,
Bibs and black bras thronging the sunshine
With hosannas of cotton and halleluiahs of wool.

THE SHORT DAYS

I like the way, in winter, cars
Ignite beneath the lingering stars
And, with a cough or two, unpark,
And roar to work still in the dark.

Like some great father, slugabed,
Whose children crack the dawn with play,
The sun retains a heavy head
Behind the hill, and stalls the day.

Then red rims gild the gutter-spouts;
The streetlamp pales; the milk-truck fades;
And housewives—husbands gone—wash doubts
Down sinks and raise the glowing shades.

The cars are gone, they will return
When headlights in a new night burn;
Between long drinks of Acheron
The thirst of broad day has begun.

SUBURBAN MADRIGAL

Sitting here in my house,
looking through my windows
diagonally at my neighbor's house,
I see his sun-porch windows;
they are filled with blue-green,
the blue-green of my car,
which I parked in front of my house,
more or less, up the street,
where I can't directly see it.

How promiscuous is
the world of appearances!
How frail are property laws!
To him his window is filled with his
things: his lamps, his plants, his radio.
How annoyed he would be to know
that my car, legally parked,
yet violates his windows,
paints them full
(to me) of myself, my car,
my well-insured '55 Fordor Ford
a gorgeous green sunset streaking his panes.

MOSQUITO

On the fine wire of her whine she walked,
Unseen in the ominous bedroom dark.
A traitor to her camouflage, she talked
A thirsty blue streak distinct as a spark.

I was to her a fragrant lake of blood
From which she had to sip a drop or die.
A reservoir, a lavish field of food,
I lay awake, unconscious of my size.

We seemed fair-matched opponents. Soft she dropped
Down like an anchor on her thread of song.
Her nose sank thankfully in; then I slapped
At the sting on my arm, cunning and strong.

A cunning, strong Gargantua, I struck
This lover pinned in the feast of my flesh,
Lulled by my blood, relaxed, half-sated, stuck
Engrossed in the gross rivers of myself.

Success! Without a cry the creature died,
Became a fleck of fluff upon the sheet.
The small welt of remorse subsides as side
By side we, murderer and murdered, sleep.

EARTHWORM

We pattern our Heaven
on bright butterflies,
but it must be that even
in earth Heaven lies.

The worm we uproot
in turning a spade
returns, careful brute,
to the peace he has made.

God blesses him; he
gives praise with his toil,
lends comfort to me,
and aërates the soil.

Immersed in the facts,
one must worship there;
claustrophobia attacks
us even in air.

CALENDAR

Toward August's end,
a hard night rain;
and the lawn is littered
with leaves again.

How the seasons blend!
So seeming still,
summer is fettered
to a solar will

which never rests.
The slanting ray
ignites migration
within the jay

and plans for nests
are hatching when
the northern nation
looks white to men.

SEAGULLS

A gull, up close,
looks surprisingly stuffed.
His fluffy chest seems filled
with an inexpensive taxidermist's material
rather lumpily inserted. The legs,
unbent, are childish crayon strokes—
too simple to be workable.
And even the feather-markings,
whose intricate symmetry is the usual glory of birds,
are in the gull slovenly,
as if God makes too many
to make them very well.

Are they intelligent?
We imagine so, because they are ugly.
The sardonic one-eyed profile, slightly cross,
the narrow, ectomorphic head, badly combed,
the wide and nervous and well-muscled rump
all suggest deskwork: shipping rates
by day, Schopenhauer
by night, and endless coffee.

At that hour on the beach
when the flies begin biting in the renewed coolness
and the backsliding skin of the after-surf
reflects a pink shimmer before being blotted,
the gulls stand around in the dimpled sand
like those melancholy European crowds
that gather in cobbled public squares in the wake
of assassinations and invasions,
heads cocked to hear the latest radio reports.

It is also this hour when plump young couples
walk down to the water, bumping together,
and stand thigh-deep in the rhythmic glass.
Then they walk back toward the car,

tugging as if at a secret between them,
but which neither quite knows;
walk capricious paths through the scattering gulls,
as in some mythologies
beautiful gods stroll unconcerned
among our mortal apprehensions.

MAPLES IN A SPRUCE FOREST

They live by attenuation,
Straining, vine-thin,
Up to gaps their gold leaves crowd
Like drowning faces surfacing.

Wherever dappled sun persists,
Shy leaves work photosynthesis;
Until I saw these slender doomed,
I did not know what a maple is.

The life that plumps the oval
In the open meadow full
Is beggared here, distended toward
The dying light available.

Maturity of sullen spruce
Will murder these deciduous;
A little while, the fretted gloom
Is dappled with chartreuse.

VERMONT

Here green is king again,
Usurping honest men.
Like Brazilian cathedrals gone under to creepers,
Gray silos mourn their keepers.

Here ski tows
And shy cows
Alone pin the ragged slopes to the earth
Of profitable worth.

Hawks, professors,
And summering ministers
Roost on the mountainsides of poverty
And sniff the poetry,

And every year
The big black bear,
Slavering through the woods with scrolling mouth,
Comes further south.

HOEING

I sometimes fear the younger generation will be deprived
  of the pleasures of hoeing;
    there is no knowing
how many souls have been formed by this simple exercise.

The dry earth like a great scab breaks, revealing
  moist-dark loam—
    the pea-root's home,
a fertile wound perpetually healing.

How neatly the green weeds go under!
  The blade chops the earth new.
    Ignorant the wise boy who
has never performed this simple, stupid, and useful wonder.

HOW TO BE UNCLE SAM

My father knew
　　how to be
　　　　Uncle Sam.

Six feet two,
　　he led the
　　　　parade

the year
　　the boys came back
　　　　from war.

Splendidly
　　spatted, his legs
　　　　like canes,

his dandy coat
　　like a
　　　　bluebird's back,

he led the parade,
　　and then
　　　　a man

(I've never been sure
　　he was honestly
　　　　canned—

he might have been
　　consciously
　　　　after a laugh)

popped
　　from the crowd,
　　　　swinging his hands,

and screamed,
    "You're the s.o.b.
        who takes

all my money!"
    and took
        a poke at

my own father.
    He missed
        by half

an inch; he felt
    the wind, my father
        later said.

When the cops
    grabbed that one,
        another man

shouted from the
    crowd in a
        voice like brass:

"I don't care if
    you take a poke at
        Updike,

but don't you
    bother
        Uncle Sam!"

Three boys, American, in dungarees,
walk at a slant across the street
against the mild slant of the winter sun,
moseying out this small, still holiday.

The back of the cold is broken; later snows
will follow, mixed with rain, but today
the macadam is bare, the sun loops high,
and the trees are bathed in sweet grayness.

He was a perfect hero: a man of stone,
as colorless as a monument,
anonymous as Shakespeare. We know him
only as the author of his deeds.

There may have been a man: a surveyor,
a wencher, a temper, a stubborn farmer's mind;
but our legends seem impertinent
gaieties scratched upon his granite.

He gazes at us from our dollar bills
reproachfully, a strange green lady,
heavy-lidded, niggle-lipped, and wigged,
who served us better than we have deserved.

More than great successes, we love great failures.
Lincoln is Messiah; he, merely Caesar.
He suffered greatness like a curse.
He fathered our country, we feel, without great joy.

But let us love him now, for he crossed the famous ice,
brought us out of winter, stood, and surveyed
the breadth of our land exulting in the sun:
looked forward to the summer that is past.

SHILLINGTON

The vacant lots are occupied, the woods
Diminish, Slate Hill sinks beneath its crown
Of solvent homes, and marketable goods
On all sides crowd the good remembered town.

Returning, we find our snapshots inexact.
Perhaps a condition of being alive
Is that the clothes which, setting out, we packed
With love no longer fit when we arrive.

Yet sights that limited our truth were strange
To older eyes; the town that we have lost
Is being found by hands that still arrange
Horse chestnut heaps and fingerpaint on frost.

Time shades these alleys; every pavement crack
Is mapped somewhere. A solemn concrete ball,
On the gatepost of a sold house, brings back
A waist leaning against a buckling wall.

The gutter-fires smoke, their burning done
Except for, fanned within, an orange feather;
We have one home, the first, and leave that one.
The having and leaving go on together.

Written for the semicentennial celebration of this borough's incorporation in 1908.

MOVIE HOUSE

View it, by day, from the back,
from the parking lot in the rear,
for from this angle only
the beautiful brick blankness can be grasped.
Monumentality
wears one face in all ages.

No windows intrude real light
into this temple of shades,
and the size of it,
the size of the great rear wall measures
the breadth of the dreams we have had here.
It dwarfs the village bank,
outlooms the town hall,
and even in its decline
makes the bright-ceilinged supermarket seem mean.

Stark closet of stealthy rapture,
vast introspective camera
wherein our most daring self-projections
were given familiar names:
stand, stand by your macadam lake
and tell the aeons of our extinction
that we too could house our gods,
could secrete a pyramid
to sight the stars by.

OLD-FASHIONED
LIGHTNING ROD

Green upright rope
of copper, sprouting
(from my perspective) from
an amber ball—jaundiced amber,
the belly-bulb
of an old grasshopper—
braced between three
sturdy curlicues of wrought
iron (like elegancies
of logical thought)
and culminating—the rod,
the slender wand of spiral
copper weathered pistachio-pale—
in a crown, a star
of five radiating thorns
honed fine on the fine-grained
grinding blue wheel of sky:
flared fingers, a torch,
a gesture, crying,
"I dare you!"

THE STUNT FLIER

I come into my dim bedroom
innocently and my baby
is lying in her crib face-down;
just a hemisphere of the half-bald head
shows, and the bare feet, uncovered,
the small feet crossed at the ankles
like a dancer doing easily
a difficult step—or,
more exactly, like a cherub
planing through Heaven,
cruising at a middle altitude
through the cumulus of the tumbled covers,
which disclose the feet crossed
at the ankles *à la* small boys who,
exulting in their mastery of bicycles,
lift their hands from the handle bars
to demonstrate how easy gliding is.

THE FRITILLARY

The fritillary,
Fickle, wary,
Flits from plant to plant with nary
A forethought as to where he
Alights, a butterfly.

And, what's extraordinary,
Is also an herb—
The same word serves.
Nothing disturbs
Its thick green nerves.

When one lights on the other it is very
Nice:
The spotted wings and the spotted petals, both
      spelled from the Latin *fritillus* [dice],
Nod together
Toward a center
Where a mirror
Might be imagined.
They are tangent,
Self to self, the same
Within a single name.
The miracle has occurred.

Alas! The wingèd word
With a blind flap leaves the leaved,
Unbereaved,
And bobbles down the breeze,
Careless of etymologies.

MOBILE OF BIRDS

There is something
in their planetary weave that is comforting.

The polycentric orbits, elliptical
with mutual motion,
random as nature, and yet, above all,
calculable, recall
those old Ptolemaic heavens small
enough for the Byzantine Trinity,
    Plato's Ideals,
    formal devotion,
seven levels of bliss, and numberless wheels
of omen, balanced occultly.

                      A small bird
at an arc's extremity
adequately weights
his larger mates'
compounded mass: absurd
but actual—there he floats!

Persisting through a doorway, shadow-casting light
    dissolves on the wall
    the mobile's threads
and turns its spatial conversation
dialectical. Silhouettes,
projections of identities,
merge and part and reunite
in shapely syntheses—

                    an illusion,
for the birds on their perches of fine wire avoid collusion
and are twirled
alone in their suspenseful world.

LES SAINTS NOUVEAUX

Proust, doing penance
in a cork-lined room,
numbered the petals
in the orchards of doom
and sighed through the vortex
of his own strained breath
the wonderfully abundant
perfume called Death.

Brancusi, an anchorite
among rough shapes,
blessed each with his eyes
until like grapes
they popped, releasing
kernels of motion
as patiently worked
as if by the ocean.

Cézanne, grave man,
pondered the scene
and saw it with passion
as orange and green,
and weighted his strokes
with days of decision,
and founded on apples
theologies of vision.

DIE NEUEN HEILIGEN

Kierkegaard, a
cripple and a Dane,
disdained to marry;
the consequent strain
unsprung the whirling
gay knives of his wits,
which slashed the Ideal
and himself to bits.

Kafka, a lawyer
and citizen of Prague,
became consumptive
in the metaphysic fog
and, coughing with laughter,
lampooned the sad state
that judged its defendants
all guilty of Fate.

Karl Barth, more healthy,
and married, and Swiss,
lived longer, yet took
small comfort from this;
Nein! he cried, roaring
in utter despair
the Credo that Culture
left up in the air.

TREES EAT SUNSHINE

It's the fact:
their broad leaves lap it up like milk
and turn it into twigs.

Fish eat fish.
Lamps eat light
and when their feast has starved their filament
go out.

So do we,
and all sweet creatures—
cats eating horses, horses grass, grass earth, earth
        water—
except for the distant Man

who inhales the savor of souls—
let us all strive to resemble this giant!

FEVER

I have brought back a good message from the land of
     102°:
God exists.
I had seriously doubted it before;
but the bedposts spoke of it with utmost confidence,
the threads in my blanket took it for granted,
the tree outside the window dismissed all complaints,
and I have not slept so justly for years.
It is hard, now, to convey
how emblematically appearances sat
upon the membranes of my consciousness;
but it is a truth long known,
that some secrets are hidden from health.

SEVEN STANZAS AT EASTER

Make no mistake: if He rose at all
it was as His body;
if the cells' dissolution did not reverse, the molecules
    reknit, the amino acids rekindle,
the Church will fall.

It was not as the flowers,
each soft Spring recurrent;
it was not as His Spirit in the mouths and fuddled
    eyes of the eleven apostles;
it was as His flesh: ours.

The same hinged thumbs and toes,
the same valved heart
that—pierced—died, withered, paused, and then
    regathered out of enduring Might
new strength to enclose.

Let us not mock God with metaphor,
analogy, sidestepping, transcendence;
making of the event a parable, a sign painted in the
    faded credulity of earlier ages:
let us walk through the door.

The stone is rolled back, not papier-mâché,
not a stone in a story,
but the vast rock of materiality that in the slow
    grinding of time will eclipse for each of us
the wide light of day.

And if we will have an angel at the tomb,
make it a real angel,
weighty with Max Planck's quanta, vivid with hair,
    opaque in the dawn light, robed in real linen
spun on a definite loom.

Let us not seek to make it less monstrous,
for our own convenience, our own sense of beauty,
lest, awakened in one unthinkable hour, we are
            embarrassed by the miracle,
and crushed by remonstrance.

Written for a religious arts festival sponsored by the Clifton Lutheran
Church, of Marblehead, Mass.

VIBRATION

The world vibrates, my sleepless nights
discovered. The air conditioner hummed;
I turned it off. The plumbing
in the next apartment sang;
I moved away, and found a town
whose factories shuddered as they worked
all night. The wires on the poles
outside my windows quivered in an ecstasy
stretched thin between horizons.
I went to where no wires were; and there,
as I lay still, a dragon tremor
seized my darkened body, gnawed
my heart, and murmured, *I am you.*

MODIGLIANI'S DEATH MASK

Fogg Museum, Cambridge

The shell of a doll's head,
It stares askew, lopsided in death,
With nervous lips, a dirty tan,
And no bigger than my hand.
Could the man have been that small?
Or is life, like rapid motion,
An enlarging illusion?
Ringed, Italianly, with ivy,
The mask makes an effect of litter,
Preserved inside its glass case like
An oddly favored grapefruit rind.

SUMMER: WEST SIDE

When on the coral-red steps of old brownstones
Puerto Rican boys, their white shirts luminous,
gather, and their laughter
conveys menace as far as Central Park West,

When the cheesecake shops on Broadway
keep open long into the dark,
and the Chinaman down in his hole of seven steps
leaves the door of his laundry ajar,
releasing a blue smell of starch,

When the indefatigable lines of parked cars
seem embedded in the tar,
and the swish of the cars on the Drive
seems urgently loud—

Then even the lapping of wavelets
on the boards of a barge on the Hudson
is audible,
and Downtown's foggy glow
fills your windows right up to the top.

And you walk in the mornings with your cool suit
sheathing the fresh tingle of your shower,
and the gratings idly steam,
and the damp path of the street-sweeper evaporates,

And—an oddly joyful sight—
the dentists' and chiropractors' white signs low
in the windows of the great ochre buildings on Eighty-
            sixth Street
seem slightly darkened
by one more night's deposit of vigil.

3 A.M.

By the brilliant ramp
of a ceaseless garage

the eye like a piece of newspaper
staring from a collage

records on a yellowing
gridwork of nerve

"policemen move on feet of glue,
sailors stick to the curb."

EROTIC EPIGRAMS

I

The landscape of love
can only be seen
through a slim windowpane
one's own breath fogs.

II

Iseult, to Tristan
(condemned to die),
is like a letter of reprieve
which is never delivered
but he knows has been dispatched.

III

Hoping to fashion a mirror, the lover
doth polish the face of his beloved
until he produces a skull.

FLIRT

The flirt is an antelope of flame,
igniting the plain
wherever she hesitates.
She kisses my wrist, waits,
and watches the flush of pride
absurdly kindle my eyes.
She talks in riddles,
exposes her middle,
is hard and strange in my arms:
I love her. Her charms
are those of a fine old book with half-cut pages,
bound in warm plush at her white neck's nape.

THE BLESSING

The room darkened, darkened until
our nakedness was a form of gray;
then the rain came bursting,
and we were sheltered, blessed,
upheld in a world of elements
that held us justified.
In all the love I had felt for you before,
in all that love,
there was no love
like that I felt when the rain began:
dim room, enveloping rush,
the slenderness of your throat,
the blessèd slenderness.

THE GREAT SCARF OF BIRDS

Playing golf on Cape Ann in October,
I saw something to remember.

Ripe apples were caught like red fish in the nets
of their branches. The maples
were colored like apples,
part orange and red, part green.
The elms, already transparent trees,
seemed swaying vases full of sky. The sky
was dramatic with great straggling V's
of geese streaming south, mare's-tails above them.
Their trumpeting made us look up and around.
The course sloped into salt marshes,
and this seemed to cause the abundance of birds.

As if out of the Bible
or science fiction,
a cloud appeared, a cloud of dots
like iron filings which a magnet
underneath the paper undulates.
It dartingly darkened in spots,
paled, pulsed, compressed, distended, yet
held an identity firm: a flock
of starlings, as much one thing as a rock.
One will moved above the trees
the liquid and hesitant drift.

Come nearer, it became less marvellous,
more legible, and merely huge.
"I never saw so many birds!" my friend exclaimed.
We returned our eyes to the game.
Later, as Lot's wife must have done,
in a pause of walking, not thinking
of calling down a consequence,
I lazily looked around.

The rise of the fairway above us was tinted,
so evenly tinted I might not have noticed
but that at the rim of the delicate shadow
the starlings were thicker and outlined the flock
as an inkstain in drying pronounces its edges.
The gradual rise of green was vastly covered;
I had thought nothing in nature could be so broad
          but grass.

And as
I watched, one bird,
prompted by accident or will to lead,
ceased resting; and, lifting in a casual billow,
the flock ascended as a lady's scarf,
transparent, of gray, might be twitched
by one corner, drawn upward and then,
decided against, negligently tossed toward a chair:
the southward cloud withdrew into the air.

Long had it been since my heart
had been lifted as it was by the lifting of that great
          scarf.

WINTER OCEAN

Many-maned scud-thumper, tub
of male whales, maker of worn wood, shrub-
ruster, sky-mocker, rave!
portly pusher of waves, wind-slave.